tHE FlaWs in Our tEEn

An Unfiltered Look at the Teenage Years Through Poetry.

sasha davis

and

r. a. Bentinck

FYAPUBLISHING | GEORGETOWN

FyaPublishing

95 South Turkeyen,

Georgetown, Guyana.

tHE Flaws Yn Our tEEN/ sasha davis and r. a. bentinck.

ISBN **978-0-9994445-4-2**

Cover design by **r. A. bentinck**

Cover image by **Alfred Anderson**

To all teenagers

When you are in your teenage years you are consciously experiencing everything for the first time, so adolescent stories are all beginnings. There are never any endings.

–AIDAN CHAMBERS

sasha davis and r. a. bentinck

Contents

Preface

The teenage years are a time of significant change and growth, both physically and emotionally. They can be a tumultuous and confusing period, full of both joy and pain. Sasha Davis and r. A. Bentinck have captured these experiences in their poetry collection, "The Flaws in Our Teen: An Unfiltered Look at the Teenage Years Through Poetry."

This collection is a raw and honest look at the struggles and triumphs of being a teenager. It explores the wide range of emotions that come with growing up, from the excitement of first love to the heartache of loss. The poems in this collection are relatable and will resonate with readers of all ages.

Davis and bentinck have a unique style of writing that is both powerful and emotive. They write about the complexities of the teenage years with a keen eye for detail and a deep understanding of the human experience. This collection is a testament to their ability to capture the essence of what it means to be a teenager in a way that is both poignant and relatable.

The reader will find themselves laughing, crying and feeling every other emotion in between as they journey through the collection. The poems in this collection are not sugar-coated, they are real and raw, providing an unfiltered look at the teenage years. They will take you on a journey through the ups and downs of growing up and make you realize that you are not alone in your experiences.

This collection is not only for teenagers but for anyone who has ever been a teenager or who has ever loved one. It is a reminder that the teenage years are a time of great growth and change, and that it is important to embrace the flaws in ourselves and in those around us.

"The Flaws in Our Teen" is a powerful and emotive collection of poetry that provides an authentic and relatable look at the teenage years. Sasha Davis and r. A. bentinck have done an excellent job of capturing the complexities of growing up in a way that is both meaningful and accessible to all readers.

This book will resonate with anyone who has ever been a teenager or loved one. It is a must-read for all.

Georgetown, Guyana.

2019.

The Faults in Our Teen

By Sasha Davis

i cover my flaws with snap filters,
i hide my emotions through
Drake's lyrics.

i empathise with lonely quotes,
i run away from tricky dealings.
the sound of commitment causes me
to shut myself away.

arrows of betrayal have pierced my heart
and agony has flooded my system.
i've been abused and mistreated under
a system of oppressive thoughts,
obsessive desires and sinful dealings.
i have been thrust into the limelight
of an unforgiving society

where the colour of my skin sickens
them and the knots of my hair tangle
and fuse their frustrations.

i am a teen of today.
looking for a way to hide her face
behind the masses of people who scream
bloody murder when they
hear her name.

i am a product of a system that
broke me, left me wondering about
my reflection for three years
tore my heart out and
humbly allowed me to watch it bleed.

 i am a teen of today.
a boy who was forcibly thrown off the
plane because of the religious songs

6

i sing the drabs that crown my head
and the mirror imperfections that
adorn my face.

i am a teen of today.
a girl who was thrown against the
scraping boots of a society that lusted
after her body who was tricked and
captured by men who took her as
their object.

i am a teen of today.
struggling to choose an identity that
suits me because of the obnoxious ideals
of my elders and outsiders who feel
they know me.

i am a teen of today.
so don't ask me why these tears gather

on the pores of my cheeks

or why my eyes have lost their twinkle.

you left me to fend against a pack

of wolves and jailed me when

i ought not conform.

i am a teen of today.

bounded to a society that

only wishes

for me to sink with it.

Pimples Paradise (hormonal imbalances)

By r. A. bentinck

my friends' faces

are smooth

as a baby's bottom,

my cheeks are

rough as an unkempt

gravelled road.

i have experimented with every

products from the

adverts on the television

still no results.

i wanna lock myself

away from life

but my parent insist

that i can't live life
that way.

the countless embarrassing
comments and
uncomfortable stares
that i have to endure
every day are like
a gorilla on my back
who refuses to get off.

my friends' faces
are smooth
as a baby's bottom,
mine is
a pimples paradise.
somebody, anybody
please,
bury me alive!

Individual

By Sasha Davis

i don't owe you my light
in your darkness.

i don't owe you
the smile that dances
above my chin just beneath
the tip of my nose.

i don't owe you
the breath from my lungs.

i don't owe you
the laughter in my soul,
the fire in my eyes,
the beat of my heart.
you don't get to have me at my best
when you discarded me

at my worst.

my heart is not your playground,
my feelings are not your playthings,
my tears are not your swimming pools,
and my mouth is not your garden.

my body is not your forest,
my fingertips are not your branches.

i don't hold roots in this world
but one of a higher calling
i'm a seed sown in rich soil
i'm an individual immersed in
my own self.

Stunned

By r. A. bentinck

she has been the source

of my happiness for

so many years.

then school closed for

the summer's vacation

and she went away.

when she returned

things were never the same,

she dodged me at all cost.

then months later

a classmate gave us the news,

Shelly is pregnant.

i was stunned into silence
as beads of tears
trickled down my parched
cheeks.

how could she do this to me?
was the lingering question
molesting my mind.

Bogeyman

By Sasha Davis

i've sat back and thought on all

the lies i was fed as a child

i remember the countless stories of

the boogeyman.

the terrifying ending that awaited if you

missed a bath, didn't brush your teeth, or if

you didn't complete your homework

on time.

i can recall every threat, lie, and

an empty promise that awaited me if

i disobeyed any rule

my mother set in place

i had yet to know that the boogeyman could

operate through people and employ them as

puppets in a string of cruel games

i lacked knowledge regarding his
authority and his hold on unspoken fears
i was ignorant of the fact that physical pain
was not the only pain
with enough coercion to make
a human being break

i would rather sit through
a thousand lashes than
undergo another disappointment,
lie across on a bed of needles to avoid
falling for another fable,

battle the gods of thunder and water
rather than entrust my heart
to someone who
deceitfully claims their love for me.

only disappointment awaits

leaving you to dwell inside desolate walls.

enabling you to disappear

but remain alert or else

the boogeyman will tear you apart.

The Juvenile in Me

By r. A. bentinck

i'm an adult mind
ambushed in a teen's body.
a revolutionary with
irrational causes,
bewildered and misguided.

fluctuating desires
that have no name
and
lots of sweethearts
who reject my
persistent game.

i am an explosive adventurer,
with invading emotions
and mercenary intentions.

an excess of vitality

and a shortage of time

and adult reality.

what a time to be alive.

i am a teenage rebel

with one goal on

my mind-

winning.

Memory

By Sasha Davis

it's been weeks since

you last called,

have you forgotten me?

i remember your long strides

through my heart and

your quick withdrawal

from my body.

it seems

somewhere along the way

you've lost me.

Sneak Away

By r. A. bentinck

the still darkness of the night

was too tempting to resist,

so we sneaked away from

the group

and found ourselves under

the watchful eyes of the stars.

we were both extremely nervous

to fully capitalise on

this ideal setting.

i was shaking like a leaf

and she was too nervous

to even look me in the eyes.

we squeezed each other's hands

and i felt the coldness

that enveloped our bodies.

i wanted to caress her

but couldn't i was

too much of a nervous wreck.

A Love Lost

By Sasha Davis

i dreamt of you again.

the way you use

to sing my name

and the way

your smile curved

delicately on your face.

i always thought

your smile would curve

in my direction

until you left.

why did you leave?

The New Girl

By r. A. bentinck

i met this girl yesterday
and when she smiled
for the first time,

i saw my future,
my gorgeous wife,
my adorable children,
and the source of
my continued happiness
in an instance.

she was the new girl
in our school
and in my class.
she was a goddess
in school uniform.

24

Pain

By Sasha Davis

my hand holds

a multitude of calluses

mirroring my heart.

The Bully's Toy

By r. A. bentinck

after this much

pounding

i might as well

be labelled as

a punching bag.

i get beat down

because i declined

to share the answer

to a test question,

i get pummelled

for not handing over

my favourite lunch,

i get beat up

because i don't

complain to my teachers

and

i get flattened

when i complained

to the teacher.

damn if i don't!

damn when i do!

let's face it,

at the end

of the day

i am

just a bully's plaything.

None

By Sasha Davis

loves light shines as bright as an emerald

when it isn't touched or defiled.

its centerpieces woven into our mouths and

planted in our hands

spoken through our very words

towards our counterpart.

love is a fickle industry many class for the

imprudent and weak-hearted

they have fallen to the corruption of the

tantalizing desire

yet the wise have spoken the very same

words and once hummed

the vivid melodies

drunk from the same cup,

embraced a warm body,

got entrapped in the sheets,

and breathed the sweet vigor

of a night of passion.

they've experienced it all

only to breathe in cold air

and release shaky breaths.

the songs have morphed into howls a

and the bitter aftertaste in the cup is noticed.

the memories become nightmares

and tomorrow becomes too much of

a burden to wake up.

the victims of imagination and cursory

heartbreak

have fallen to the trap of fantasies

casting away the realities in store.

the absence of a lover

has become a usual occasion

and the sensual nights have ceased.

no lingering kiss can replace the touch,

or feeling a beautiful rose such as love can

imprint on the human heart

My First Joint

By r. A. bentinck

i am going

to cough up my lung

anytime now!

by the time that happens

i will be too blind

to see it or find it.

with runny eyes,

lungs that are

on fire

and an

unwelcomed cough

that refuses to disappear.

i keeled over

in a daze.

i feel berated

by the taunting grin

and enquiring eyes

of my puzzled friends.

the smoke-clogged room

has dim the daylight

out of my moment

and i swear that

death is speedily approaching.

these are some

of the forgettable memories

that came with the smoking

of my first joint.

I Miss Him

By Sasha Davis

i miss him.

i miss everything about him.

the way his lips curved up into a smile

his eyes

the delicate words he used to whisper.

i miss him.

the touch of his hands

on my skin

the air of protection he provided

the safety net he seemed to

always have.

i miss him.

his voice

his laugh
his confident attitude.

i miss him.

but his thoughts never run by any of his
wilted flowers.

Cindy

By r. A. bentinck

she was

a sensational subject

but our verbs never agreed.

she was

tall and gracefully elegant,

and walked like

a natural model

on the catwalk.

she made the cheap-looking

school uniform

looked expensive and

her effervescent personality

made us felt like we all had a chance.

she was the apple of our

teenage eyes,

in the prime of puberty

when we were all

hyped up on hormones

and female fantasies.

she wore a smile that

broke our hearts but

when she shared it with us,

we felt like kings.

she was a constant distraction in class

as our imaginations often wondered

to dreamy places with her

at the center of it all.

Cindy wreaked havoc on

the fragile emotions of

all the teenage boys

in her class.

she was so close

yet far beyond our reach.

Sixteen

By Sasha Davis

embarking on another journey seemed
scary i had just embraced being fifteen
i never imagined the great emphasis i
placed on adding a year onto my life.

i had escaped the clutches of immaturity
i had now come face to face with the
new impediments of life.

the pressures that are conclusive of
having low self-esteem, arising health
problems and a haunting past would
only seem to become greater with a
another year added to my life.

i seem to have been losing at every
point and quickly crumbling under

38

the pressure of this picture that is painted
around maturity.

what people and magazines fail to tell
you is that meeting this new found
maturity is not always as glamorous as
you've pictured it.

now that i'm sixteen i can officially say
that i am still growing
and learning when it comes to
everything life presents to me on a
deceptive highly decorated platter.

i still look in the mirror and inspect
every flaw, and a scar that paints its way
from the tip of my head to my chin
the illusion of the perfect high-school
boyfriend still is scorched in my mind

along with with the many dents that illusion
brought.

the memory and reality of a broken girl
still embodies me
i am still the lost girl who is constantly
fighting to have a boldness that draws
in onlookers but i still remain a bunny
in a den of lions. still timid
and most times passive.

and i am still learning that it's okay to
be flustered allowing myself
to grow without the speed limits
and timers i tried to place on it.

there is a certain beauty about a
wandering teenager because even the
most mature adults are inwardly still

scared teenagers.

Someday-Ms Impatient

By r. A. bentinck

someday,

a young man will get lost

just looking into your eyes.

someday,

a young man will sing

to the heavens just

because he found your love.

someday,

a young man will have the

privilege to sit in the company

of your smile.

someday,

one sensible young man will treat you

like the queen you are-
just like royalty.

someday,
you will come to realise
your true value,
and you will never settle for
anything but the best.

someday,
your garden will bloom
with beautiful roses
and the rain will fall just for you.

someday,
you will find a way
to smile through the pouring rain.

someday,

it will all get easier.

someday,
it will all make sense.

someday,
you will have the answers
to the difficult questions
and the solutions
to the unsolvable problems.

someday,
just be patient.

Ugly

By Sasha Davis

i could tell,

when their eyes slid off of me

their mouths screwed up in disgust

the silent whispers and snide comments

the ridicule

the look of disdain.

i could always tell

when they lied

disguising the selfish gain

with genuine interest.

the way their eyes dissected me

i could tell, always

the discussions concerning

different girls.

i could tell,

but one day soon i won't be able to tell

because the beating will cease

and a plethora of rest will envelop me

hurt will be as foreign as i am

to this life.

i will dance with the stars and

slide off the moon

and sleep on the clouds

bliss

yes bliss

is the only thing i'll know.

The Emotional Rollercoaster

By r. A. bentinck

it ain't fun

nor

it ain't funny.

this is a rollercoaster.

one time you are in

another time you are out.

one time

you are up

another time

you are down.

one moment

you are laughing

another moment

you are crying.

if it's not me,

it's a friend

i just don't understand

these teenage days.

You Don't Know Her

By Sasha Davis

it angers me that so many people
claimed that they knew her
understood her
mourned with her
when they are ignorant of what she
believed, or fought for.

they didn't
recognize the fake smile that played on
her lips, or the way her eyes gradually
got dimmer over time.
they looked at the surface,
and barely glanced at the roots.

they chose to hear genuine laughter
when in actuality she was one more tear
away from crumbling

they decided to focus on her galling
tendencies instead of wondering if it
was her way of covering up a hidden scar.

don't you dare cry at her funeral
because the truth is you never knew her.
you choose to study a version of her
that suited your interest temporarily,
not who she really was.

don't cry for a girl you barely know
because how can you truly mourn when
you don't even know what you've lost?

Conversations with a Young Girl

By r. A. bentinck

she is a natural beauty

in so many ways,

but

all that flows from her mouth

is self-hatred.

how do you talk to a young girl

who cannot see her value and self-

worth?

she still has her angelic

newborn eyes

and a smile that glows with joy

but the words that emanate

from her mouth

are like a dagger

to her tender heart.
how do you talk to a young girl
who cannot see her natural beauty?

society's standard is all she knows
and her naturalness
her mirror keeps rejecting.

she feels neglected,
unloved,
hated,
discarded.

her complexion is too chocolate,
her hair too kinky and unruly,
she just doesn't fit in.

how do you convince a young girl
that her uniqueness is a gorgeous

blessing?

there is no hatred

like self-hatred,

and she has a surplus of this stuff.

my heart bleeds for her,

my logical arguments

and sensible reasoning

is not penetrating the fortress of her

made up mind.

"i'm not pretty!"

she keeps reminding me

for the umpteenth time.

my persuasive bank account

is now-bankrupt on her.

how do you talk to a young girl

who cannot see her value and self-worth?

can someone tell me,

please?

I Wasn't Her

By Sasha Davis

what made you

fall in love with her?

was it the way she smiled

through her eyes?

or

the waves that rippled

through her hair?

was it the scent that decorated

the air as she left?

what made you fall into her?

the musical note edged in her throat

the laugh that echoed off inside

of your heart

or

the simple assets

such as

her neatly clipped nails,

plump lips,

and

tempting figure.

it must've been

something i didn't have

or

something i didn't perfect.

i was willing to be

on points just

to deserve your affection

but you forgot to leave

a little note saying

i wasn't her.

The It Girl

By r. A. bentinck

i could never discern

the notion of

"she is out of your league"

what do you mean?

how is that possible?

i hook up with her

on so many levels

so regularly in

my imagination!

the tensions that

suddenly

flares up at the sight of her,

the arousal of my senses

and sensuous faculties,

the regular dosage

of daydreams with her

in the spotlight consistently.

how can she

be out of my league?

Heartache

By Sasha Davis

the feeling of anguish

regret

and sorrow all plague me relentlessly

eating away at my fragile visage

my heart is restricted by a constant ache

that accompanies it every time.

i see you smile

joy flees taking cover

shielding itself off from you.

the thought of leaving has my very soul

entrapped in anger and

an overwhelming sense of sorrow

haunts me

choking me to the point where

the air feels constricted every time i try to

remind me to inhale and exhale.

tears fall one by one down my cheek
late into the night as i remember every
real and made up moment we shared
how can i leave a piece of my heart here
when i've never felt so whole?

the burning in my chest justifies all
reckless thought of telling you
how i feel, however
the fear of rejection still
lingers in the background restricting me
from giving you all of me.

instead, i gave you bits and
pieces of my heart.
questions of my appearance, or my
intelligence stop me completely

silencing me with an overwhelming

feeling of shame

keeps the truth enclosed in my heart.

all the sound advice i shout at

the screen in romantic movies are forced

away and forgotten regarded as nothing

but odd blurs.

i plaster on a fake smile with

a joyous atmosphere

surrounding me and i fight

back against the whirlwind of

emotions i feel.

i ignore it all and securely store it away

gently ignoring the tears that brim my

eyes every time you look at me.

so, i whisper my final goodbye to you

under my breath cancelling every new
and unfamiliar emotion that you
brought when you came into my life.

the knowledge of our season coming
to an end still haunts me,
but the ghost of a smile and
the hopeful spirit you
ignited in me will always be
engraved in my mind
you added to me and
i will always love you for that.

The Juggler

By r. A. bentinck

yesterday i was

was sifting through

the gossips of

my best friends.

today i am dealing with

a pocket full

of vicious self-criticism.

tomorrow i will

be negotiating

the taunts

of countless critics

who have been whetting

their words

standing by for

the slaughter.

Drowning

By Sasha Davis

i'm submerged in lies and doubts that

constantly come at me with weapons in

the form of daggers from

every different direction

being yanked mercilessly

away from the shoreline.

my arms flailing and exhaustion

reaching its peak with

no boat to shield me,

and no sailor to guide me.

stranded in the middle of this vast

ocean in an abundance of waves of

doubt and fear relentlessly trying

to overtake me and

disrupt my path brimming with

anxiety and regret aligning the harsh

waters of concern and questions

that no ordinary man can answer

with nowhere to turn and no place to

take cover i drift aimlessly

in search of land

and food to satisfy my hunger, and

fresh water to quench my thirst.

a voice is trying to call out to me from

afar to walk across the belligerent seas

that entrap me

keeping me at bay away from anything

that seems great

i'm too scared;

too fragile;

too broken;

too lost;

to even comprehend the request of

something that is greater than me
that is truly greater than all of us.

a purpose i sometimes feel is truly
more than i can bear accompanied with
disheartening trials.
i want to feel something
to experience something other than
another piercing pain in my chest or
an overwhelming sense of blinding shame.

my cold heart deprived of life,
joy;
peace;
serenity;
hope;
strength;
boldness;
laughter;

is longing to be revived, to be shocked
by a jolt of electricity to awaken it from
a slumber it was forced into six years
ago.

but for now, i'm stuck in the middle of
the ocean without a sailor and no boat
just floating aimlessly across
an unforgiving ocean being tossed and
submerged into the rough waters that
have yanked me from the shore.

Memories of Mommy

By r. A. bentinck

in the tranquillity of my room

on this sunny day

they erupted.

a gush of memories of my mother.

my peaceful mindset

disappears

and i am strangled by

powerful emotions.

my eyes are blinded as they drown

in a tsunami of tears.

my room is now crowded with

a plethora of her delicious memories.

i am swimming to survive these

   memories of mommy.

i have crossed many rivers,
and negotiated a multitude of
life's perils,
but the memories of my mother
feel like am swimming upstream.

she taught me a lot,
she showed me how to love,
she taught me how to be tough,
but i can't remember a lesson
on how to deal with her memories.
i am struggling to survive these
   memories of mommy.

i stand in the middle of my room
now flooded with these memories:
the joyful sounds of family time
ring in my ears,
i can smell the deliciousness

of her kitchen,

i can hear her melodious singing voice
lightening up the atmosphere,
i can feel her warm embrace.
they all used to make me smile
but today,
am a drowning man trying to clutch
at my sanity as i am carried away by
these unbearable
memories of mommy.

<u>Thoughts</u>

By Sasha Davis

one

two

three

the gun goes boom

slicing through the air

then through me.

three

two

one

my eyes close thirsting for the rest that

it had long been denied.

one

two

three

peace from this black hole called life.

four

five

six

to a burning abyss.

six

five

four

met with a sinister,

but beautiful visage

no ordinary man,

but a beast who ended it all

stole my soul,

killed my joy, and

destroyed my hope

used his words as weapons,

and his charm as armor

with his alluring wit

and persuasive speech i followed

little did i know

it would lead me

further away from myself

but i was blinded

by his captivating smile,

and his cool demeanor

i fell right into him

abandoning all common knowledge,

or train of thought

many people talk about mistakes.

seven

eight

nine

he was mine

ten

the difference is that

mine killed me.

Asking for a Friend

By r. A. bentinck

have you ever

fell in love with

that person so passionately

only to find out

you were just another

name to be ticked off

in their black book?

have you?

i am just inquiring for a friend.

have you ever

rejected your parents or adult

advice and poured

your heart out

into a relationship simply

to have

the jerk break your heart,

weeks or months later.

then you have to deal with

the reality of facing your parents,

seeing that look in their eyes

and knowing exactly

what they are thinking?

have you?

i am asking for a friend.

have you ever boasted

to the adults that

you know what you are

doing and you are

quite capable of dealing

with any consequences

only to fail in an epic way.

now shame chain

you to your bed

and padlock

the door of your room

where you are wishing

it will all dissipate

after the day is over.

have you?

just asking for a friend.

Nobody

By Sasha Davis

she lost her smile

and tried to find it

within friends

when that failed

she looked to boys

none ever paid attention

or saw her as pretty

but just as she was branded,

a nobody.

none saw her inner beauty

or her pained smiles

but they read her label

as a nobody each time

many tears fell

and her smile

did not return.

she craved for her father

to call her pretty

but that dream was nothing but a blur

she felt lost with

no one to turn to

not one trick in her book

she decided to place herself in a box

secured with a firm lock

to which eventually killed her spirit,

and stole her light.

she leaned on God during

her period of weakness

scared

fragile

she started to regain her strength

become stronger

in a determined quest to kill

her inner self which was filled with
an overpowering sense of doubt
which eventually dwindled to
a cruel monster made from self-hate.

finally, she accepted all hope was lost
with no one to love her
or hear her mournful cries
so, she wrote this poem
and closed her eyes
drifting off into a troubled slumber
wondering why she even wakes up
sometimes.

Isolation

By r. A. bentinck

persons don't understand me,

i can lock myself away

in my bedroom for days

and only surface for food.

i can get lost in hours of

video gaming and the rest of

the world can burn

for all i care.

i love being alone with my thoughts,

i enjoy my solitary company,

i can survive without friends

and family

at this point in my life.

just let me be.

Consumed

By Sasha Davis

consumed by the frustrations of a life

that was forced upon me

tired of the choices that never seem to

reflect my wants.

seeking direction, or a quick escape

constantly pouring salt on past wounds

relishing in the sting of pain it brings

hoping that it gets so difficult that i

muster up the courage to finally

end it all.

done with life's empty words,

and thoughtless actions

fed up with the pain that has been

exerted on me from a stolen childhood

searching for someone who cares

repeatedly asking God if he can

hear me

can you hear me,

God?

The First Time

By r. A. bentinck

the first time

i kissed her

i can remember going

wild with excitement

after she left.

i could feel the softness

of her lips telling

me how much

she loves me,

i could feel

her soft breath

caressing my skin

and

in the middle

of all the excitement

one question flashed

across my mind-

did i do it right?

Women's Day

By Sasha Davis

they told me i was

too loud,

too aggressive,

and too curious.

that i should talk less and listen more.

i should be seen, but not heard.

to cover up myself, and hide what i

really stand for.

so, i listened for a while.

i dressed a certain way and kept my

mouth shut.

i speak when spoken to and only gave

my opinion when asked.

today i say

"goodbye"

to every chain, they tried to bound me

with.

"no"

to every ignorant phrase that emerged

from their mouths.

and

"stay strong"

to every girl who was placed in a box.

we are the lights of this world,

and through God's grace, we will

continue to push for equality.

Crush on You

By r. A. bentinck

with my boys,

i'm a bragging authority

about the way i feel

about her

but

when she saunters by

i am like a ceased up old engine

that was neglected for years

in extreme weather condition.

embarrassing butterflies

dominates my chest

and my desires

are like an energetic Pitbull

on uncertain leach.

i'm a pathetic sight

overwhelmed by

my weak energies.

I Loved You

By Sasha Davis

i loved you
with every little shattered piece, i had left.

i fought for you when you didn't care
enough to fight for me.

i defended you and lost
all sense of reason just to justify
every selfish crime you committed.

in return,
you broke my heart and left
me alone to pick up the pieces
but how do you fix a broken heart which
has already been temporarily mended a
countless number of times before
you ran when i needed you most and

ignored my desperate pleas for comfort
and carried on with life as if nothing
had happened.

my burdens doubled and my soul now
dead leaving me with an insufficient
amount of strength left to at least try
i don't have the strength
to fake a smile anymore.

i don't want to
i can't
i refuse to and choose instead
the winding path of pity and the endless
walk way of self-hate.

i decided to write my own never ever
after mocking the romantic that died
when you left

no happily ever after insight just silent
whispers of lies that scream i love you.

relentlessly demanding the opportunity
to be heard, but a cunning voice
whispers how can you love something
you carelessly tossed aside like a child
does to a broken toy.

i gather my pieces and i drown them
refusing to acknowledge any existence,
or trace of a cardiac muscle
you closed the door on us, so i tortured
myself setting fire to the door that may
have held me.

Falling for Love Again

By r. A. bentinck

am back at

this place again,

i have fallen

for love

once more.

this time she came

dressed as

the most beautiful

young girl

in our school.

she was sweet

and polite and

seem to only

have eyes for me.

so here i am falling

for what my mom

describes as

'puppy love.'

my days are brighter,

i smile more often

and there is always

the excitement in my eyes

when i hear

the mention of her name.

she made me fall

for this love thing again

i hope it isn't like

the short lived ones

in my past.

One More Chance

By Sasha Davis

i gave life one more chance
i attempted to try happiness
one more time.

i decided to fight despite
not having anything left.

i gave my heart and trust to a devil
who took it with a smile
and used me until he was done
then discarded me into a pile.

my trust is done and my tolerance gone
maybe it's better to go through life not
trusting anyone at all
so i'll keep my walls up and
my exterior hard

never letting anyone come too close,
or look too long.

life has failed me for the last time and
threw away all of its chances
all life ever did was destroy
a hopeless romantic.

The Sari Princess

By r. A. bentinck

all the boys told me the story.
her daddy has a gun and
her three brothers
sharpen cutlass for breakfast
every morning.

they all drool with admiration
from miles away,
and have become adroit at
throwing suave words to the wind,
hoping she will hear them.

me, i'm an infatuated prisoner and
i cared less about the shackles of fear.

she slowed down as i called out to her.
her sari flowed with the rhythm of
her tassa waist.

her smile glowed like the flames of

burning incense.

my initial words get muffled

by trepidation that berates

my courageous heart.

her soothing greetings calmed

my rapid heartbeat that was

overpowering the noise of the street.

we walked

we talked

and shared butterfly glances.

as we leisurely approached her home,

a still small voice screamed,

"are you crazy?!"

and i recalled the story

the boys told me.

her daddy has a gun and

her three brothers

sharpen cutlass for breakfast

every morning.

<u>Who Am I?</u>

By Sasha Davis

a girl with a fake smile

empty laugh

and tired eyes

the girl with

a dingy jacket

worn-out shoes

and unruly hair

the ghost of a girl who

runs from a mirror

a hopeful pessimistic

one who doesn't know how to truly

admit their feelings

i am the ghost of a girl who

conforms to an unreasonable, almost

comical standard to fit in

one that never truly has an identity

but harnesses the one that was given to
me

i am the girl who
is branded as ugly
foreign to the word beautiful

the one who strangers eyes slide off of
disgust evident in their sight
i don't know who i am except
the warped version of who the world has
designated me to be

a forgotten member of society soon to
be suicide victim taken by
the disease of no identity.

A Lifetime

By r. A. bentinck

i can

spend an eternity

on the phone with her.

her girlie voice

has a way of carrying

me away in a love rapture.

it feels so good

locked away in my room

with her on the other end of

the telephone line

i can

live a lifetime here with her.

Load

By Sasha Davis

one day you're going

to look at the sky

and finally, see

the stars

the air will become a little easier

to intake

and the load will feel a whole lot

lighter.

that's the day you'll finally be able to

wake up without

the lump in your throat

from last night's nightmares.

no more

mascara stained cheeks

no more

strained breathing

just peace.

The Melanin Princess
(for Sasha)

By r. A. bentinck

she has the eyes of an angel

with a smile that warms the

coldest of hearts

and laughter

that shatters sadness.

i hope she knows how beautiful she is.

when peer pressure barks at her heel

and critics throw darts at her face

to spoil her essence,

i hope she knows

it's ok to separate from the masses

and never yield to conformity.

on those days when her bright eyes

get cloudy

and her smile is smeared by

the burdens of gloom,

i hope she knows that

she has the power

to change and rearrange.

when the world gets tough and

friendly faces suddenly

mutate into monsters,

i hope she knows that

she is strong enough.

and when that day comes

for her to leave

her parent's nest to cleave,

i hope she knows that she is not just

a melanin princess,

but a queen in waiting.

i hope she knows.

Imagination

By Sasha Davis

i see you

out of the corner

of my eye

oh wait,

that's the depths

of my conscious

curating an image

of you again.

Swimming Lessons

By r. A. bentinck

don't be alarmed

this was the norm

for us none swimmers.

we would accompany

our brothers and their friends

on their swimming adventures

in the forbidden river.

and as always

most of us sat on the safe side of

the river bank or

for those who felt courageous

the treacherous bridge.

we watched in admiration

as they demonstrated their swimming
skills while they frolic
and horseplay with each other
in the dark water.

and when they got
tired and bored
their attention turned to us.
the little boys with
'swift feet' and 'nuff mouth.'

they perused us
like hunters.
sometimes the faster runners
manage to elude the chasing pack
while the slow runners
were always caught.

the chasing pack was

well-coordinated,

they were too many chasers

and most of us invariable

got caught because

we became tired.

the captured were brought back

kicking and screaming

with no heed given

to our loud and desperate pleas.

we were brought to the middle

of the bridge and suddenly

the river transformed into an ocean.

with hands and feet held

by two captors we were

swung like a swing in the park.

ONCE...

TWICE...

and on the THIRD swing

toss high

and far to the center of

the deep river

with a parting instruction

to swim to the edge.

on the first occasion

i was tossed

i remember going down

the first time

and i saw my world

flashed before my trepid eyes,

i resurfaced moments later

feet kicking,

and

hands splashing water.

i was screaming in fear

but none of it helped me
or earned any help or sympathy
from the skilled swimmers
looking on.

and within seconds
the river seems to suck me
below again for
the second time,
on this occasion, i swear i saw my
mother bawling at my funeral.
but somehow i surfaced again
from this watery torture.
this time i heard my brothers
and his friends shouting,
swim! swim!

i was trying my best to no avail
and as i was about to

go below for

the third time

to drink more water and

die for sure

i felt the gentle hands

of my big brother

holding me around my waist

reassuring me that i will be ok.

he held me while he swam

to the shallow side of

the river's edge.

when we got there

i was instructed

to hold on to the grass

on the bank of the river and

practicing my kicking

and floating skills.

my heart was pounding

i was existing on the limited breath

i started vomiting

river water like a pipe

while my other brothers

and their friends were

having a healthy laugh

at the whole episode.

for some unexplained reason

we accompanied them

on these swimming escapades

every time despite knowing

our fragile fate.

after repeated exposure

to being tossed in

the middle of the river,

coupled with my

practice sessions in

the shallow portion

it all eventually paid off.

i gradually learned to swim.

Hurt

By Sasha Davis

do you know what happens when
an airplane that is free-falling from the sky
hits a rough and desolate surface?

do you know what happens when
an empty heart tries to fill a broken one?

do you know what happens when a tornado
meets a hurricane?

we happened
we ran full force into each other and
never made it out breathing.

it's like we are constantly grasping for
air and trying to collect jagged pieces of

pieces and pieces we should've missed

but we collided and

no burst of colour erupted

we fell prey to our selfish desires and it

killed us both.

<u>Touched (for that young girl)</u>

By r. A. bentinck

after a while
i sensed something wasn't right.
she was so blessed with natural beauty
but she couldn't see it from
behind stained eyes.

somedays she carried herself
like a dirty rag doll,
on other days she was
the excited princess with
a skip in her steps and
sparkles in her eyes.

i worried in silence
and enquired with cautious
but probing questions.
she was always guarded.

her answers kept me at
arm's length.

a multiplicity of
fluctuating emotions and
and contrasting personalities
always give me sneak peeks
but never enough to form a
concrete conclusion.

then one day…
one day
she mustered up the courage to
summon me to an impromptu meeting.
and she told me her story.

"he touched me
inappropriately."
her eyes were glazed with

that familiar dreary look.
that always concerned me.

"he stole my innocence,
i am no longer pure!"
her voice was tainted
with hurt and regret.

"he touched me!"
it was always her dream to
save herself for that special someone.

she wanted to savour those first
moments:
her first butterfly moments,
her first kiss,
her first moments of amorous bliss.
"he stole it all from me!"
her trust in boys and meaningful

relationships have been destroyed.

her ability to see her

natural beauty objectively

is shattered!

all because he touched her

inappropriately.

R.A.P.E.

By Sasha Davis

your fevered hands searched me
as if (it contained the answers to your
nightmares) you were searching for a
spark of light in the darkness.

your eyes explored like a lion
who's meal was long overdue
your lips were pinned keeping in
the multitude of perverted thoughts your
mind carried.

your harsh ragged breaths spread
roughly around my neck paralyzing me
in fear
but who gave you the authority
the upmost permission to take me
until you were satisfied?

who gave you the right to continue as i
relentlessly pushed your hand away?

what power did you possess far beyond
human moral that encouraged you to
rub against me while my innocence
leaked away?

who whispered such violent thoughts
in your ears? convincing you i'd be
the perfect dummy to utilize
never did the word okay escape my
jagged cries.
but i suppose no never managed to
peek its scared frame out either
rushed hands angered thoughts
polluted mind ever gone innocence.

The Sleep Over

By r. A. bentinck

this is where

the booze and imagination

runs free.

this is where classmates

get freaky and wild

with excitement.

this is where we give

free reign to our teenage fantasies.

our rich classmate parents will

be out of town for a few days

so we have the mansion

to ourselves.

Loss

By Sasha Davis

losing is such a harsh reality for
so many
you are running an unfair race against
others who seem to have years of
experience compared to your
beginning steps.

you're constantly looking at others
wondering when you'll get that far or
reach that point.

but you're stuck in a continuous state of
depression you've grown comfortable
in playing the victim that becoming
the victor seems too much of a struggle
complaining seems more fruitful
than fighting.

125

this is a state many of us are stuck in
we've grown so accustomed to finishing
last that we forgot the thrill in ending
up first
settling for less than what we can give
seems more appealing than seeking
more producing more.

blaming others became so easy so
quickly that examining ourselves never
became an important task
self-discovery is replaced with fear of
knowing who you've become
the pain of not being able to do has now
outweighed what you've done
suddenly it's become years since you've
been able to relax in
the once comfortable image you've had.

the weight of having nothing becomes
something that's beginning to whether you
coming up in last has been the death to
many and will continue to kill a lot more.

The Clique

By r. A. bentinck

it's dreadful enough

that i am not

part of their flock

but

their nasty whispers

and switchblade mockery

cuts me in places

unseen.

their judgemental

eyes exposed my discomfort

in the crowd

and

their clamorous laughter

exposes my frailty

in an uncomfortable manner.

Invisible

By Sasha Davis

you saw me

when no one else did

you pointed me out of a large crowd

decided i was the ripest apple on your

tree and put me in your basket

you pinned me on top of your

Christmas tree and whispered

sweet nothings in my ear.

you saw me.

to you, i wasn't invisible

i was the raw material for your

sculpture the first draft of your book

i was a treasure intending to be crafted

to fit your design

a pearl undeserving of anyone's grasp

sometimes even yours.

129

so what changed?

you got bored

and suddenly i was attainable

there was no more lustre to me.

i kept running and you stopped chasing

you used to keep up

now all of a sudden you're lost

behind the trees, there is no trace of you

alongside me and suddenly

i'm intangible again.

you used to spot me from a great

distance follow my coconut scent

anywhere and i was unmasked

then you decided to follow the trail of

another suddenly i was.

i was too much of a burden to bear

forced to be removed from our garden

any welcome or warm greetings were
no longer awarded to me.

the softness and strength behind your
touch was no longer mine to yearn after
i was microscopic again.

another inconceivable memory
and one final reminder of what we once
were but now you've made new memories
and none of them spoke of me.

Fitting In

By r. A. bentinck

try the thing boy,
it's not that awful
it wouldn't poison you.
try the thing.

i am circled

by an overabundance of

supporting chants

while i battle my demons:

satisfying my boys

and at the same moment

trying to keep my family's

noble code of conduct intact.

the chiding expressions of

my mom resonates

in my minds

while visions
of my tough father
shot by amid
the continued barrage
of shouts,

try the thing boy,
it's not that dangerous
it wouldn't kill you.
try the thing.

Definition

By Sasha Davis

how do you define yourself?
what is the importance of this common
phrase?
the taunting nature behind is almost
too amusing to ignore.
has anyone figured out what their
personal definition of this term even is
as yet?

was it purposely set up to mock
the existence of confused teenagers,
lost adults,
and people who tend to drift
towards the shadows
this question puts us in a box called
"unclassified."
we aren't allowed to know how we feel

134

unless it suits societal preferences.
we are supposed to be a generation of
fighters, conquerors, and game-changers
but we're barely surviving
constantly losing an inner battle of self
confidence and identity
we can't help but drift.
the real question is where or
who do we drift to?

who do we run to when we are
confused, lost, angry, or upset?
when many of us can't turn to family,
or friends for comfort we don't know
what a support system really is.
it's as if we are fighting a losing battle
where the odds were purposely placed
against us
Christians look to Jesus.

Muslims look to Allah.
who does the undecided look to?

who are we?
what defines us?
what will comfort us when we can't
look at our parents, our friends, or the
people we manipulate ourselves into
believing that love us?

for scholars what do they run to when
their grades hit the floor and they break
inside?
if we can't find ourselves and our
strengths then who are we?
what defines us?

are we the ones involuntarily chosen
to be cast to the dogs?

136

i will define myself as undecided
because i fit the category and labels
associated with it.

my definition parallels insignificance
and insufficiency to people who
disregard me so easily
then it shifts to a fleeting sense of
confidence for a tiny fraction of a second
which is gone far too quickly.
to define oneself you have to know
who you are and escape
the category of unclassified.

Meet My New Friend

By r. A. bentinck

i withdraw from

my friends just

to be in his company.

sweet sleep doesn't come

easily anymore,

he keeps me up

at nights sorting through

scary thoughts.

my once excellent

grades start to

slip gradually

from A to B to C

now i am identified

as a D student.

i feel so at ease

and at home

in his company

but my other friends

and family don't

feel the same

about him.

come,

meet my new friend,

Mr depression.

Melanin Princess

By Sasha Davis

the kinky knots of your hair

the air of superiority

that surrounds you.

the fullness of your physique

and curve of your lips down

to the sway of your hips.

the seductress that abides in you and

seeps through your eyes

sliding off your lashes.

the strength of a goddess held within

the palm of your hands

life's answers are bridged by your

mouth.

the cut of your tongue

140

and the soothing tone of your voice

the passion for sincere justice in your

speech and the awareness of

the power you radiate in your walk.

the scorched memories of the stolen

lives living in your thoughts.

slaves we were taught to be

slaves we were forced to be

slaves we were demanded to be

the same truth in a different way.

but a panther stalks and preys on truth

she glides elegantly to

the beat of nature's drum

her crown urging her on,

reminding her of who she is

the looks of mistrust enlightening her

141

of what she used to be.

she marches with a purpose

and her diligence and intelligence

breech through

she's the captivator

for she is

a panther,

a warrior,

and

a ferocious fighter.

she is a phenomenal black woman.

Run Away

By r. A. bentinck

they call it *puppy love*

but we know its love-

a pure and simple love.

they said that we are too

young to understand

being so deeply in love.

so we are formulating

a plot to run away

with each other.

our parents are a constant

source of pressure and

our friends are no different.

we are going to

run away

together.

we know what we feel inside,

we know what we feel

when we are with each other.

we just want to

run away

to be free from all the pressures.

These Broken Feelings

By Sasha Davis

i woke up

with thoughts of you

again.

but i'll do

what i always do.

write you out

of my heart until

i can't feel you

in my lungs

anymore.

Do You Know?

By r. A. bentinck

do you know

what it feels like

not to have

your father around?

no one to watch you

at your ball games.

no male figure

to look up to.

no one to teach

you how to be

a young man.

do you know

what that feels like?

do you?

146

you sit alone

in a mundane and

lonely world while

your friends bond

with their fathers

and

you sit there alone

thinking

where is my daddy?

<u>Longing</u>

By Sasha Davis

why do

all my thoughts

start and end

with you?

The Crush

By r. A. bentinck

my heart is going

to leap out of my chest!

there she was sitting

in the desk right behind me.

she is

the girl of my wildest

teenage dreams,

she is more than

the apple of my eyes,

she is also

my sweetest cutie pie.

damn, my heart is

going wild

i hope she can't

hear its heavy beat

and my fast-paced breathing.

Closed Chapter

By Sasha Davis

i can see it

in your eyes.

your eyes

no longer

searched for me.

Curfew

By r. A. bentinck

the party was lit,
the DJ was killing it
with every selection
and the girls were extremely attractive
beyond belief.

we were all in the partying mood
so we got carried away by
the moment's unbridled excitement
they didn't have any curfew time
but i did.
and when i checked my watch
it was already 2 A.M.
what!
that was way past the 11 P.M.
that my father set.

all of a sudden the music
tasted sour,
my dancing waist tightened
and the girl i was dancing with
seem like a ghostly blur.

what plausible excuse can
i come up with to save
myself from a first-class ass whopping?

Walk Into Love

By r. A. bentinck

the experience boys

always told us,

never fall in love,

always walk into love.

it's the safest way to

prevent heartbreak.

i heeded their matured advice

and walked carefully into

love with her

yet here i am picking up

pieces of my heart

from off the filthy floor.

where is the wisdom in

this advice?

Coldness

By Sasha Davis

running through hills

and valleys just to see you.

bracing storms

and heavy rains

to feel

the beat of your heart.

dodging

a sense of belonging

just to be with you.

discarding

warmth and protection

to lie next to you.

if i have to bare

the cold

it is all i'll ever feel

just to be near you.

After School

By r. A. bentinck

it's always the highlight of

our school day.

the three miles walk home.

it's the time we treasure

the most.

we get to laugh and talk

and frolic with pebbles,

hold each other's hands

momentarily,

we get to feel the cooling

afternoon breeze in

the sweltering heat.

it's always the highlight of

our school day

those afternoon stroll home

and the refreshing emotions

that flows between us.

<u>Fading Away</u>

By Sasha Davis

it's a scary feeling

when you feel yourself

fading away

your heartbeat

slows down

your body

grows cold

and

you feel as if

you are sinking

but

then you begin

to realise you're just

losing your soul.

The Guidance Councellor

By r. A. bentinck

she was very convincing

with her persuasive words

and i opened like a book

and she read me thoroughly.

weeks later bits and pieces

of the intimate stories

i shared with her

started making their rounds

around the school

and the bullies got

a whiff of it.

now i am at their mercy.

i trusted the guidance counsellor

now she has my problems

all over the school

she damaged my already

fragile trust and emotions.

<u>Sky</u>

By Sasha Davis

i saw you when

i looked at the sky

through the wispy clouds

i saw

the glimpse

of your eyes peek out

the bright blue

of the intriguing sky

reminds me

of the blood

in your veins-

cold.

the wispy clouds

that form

a different shape

for all who are entrapped

by its beauty

remind me of how

you let me

fall through you.

faulty

the shy sun

that allowed

the clouds to protect

it's lower half

reminded me

of your eyes

that i let

lead me

into darkness.

manipulating

i find you

in the sky

and i catch a glimpse

of you

when i close my eyes

do i leave

little messages

when you see me?

The Cougar

By r. A. bentinck

she ensnared me by surprise
i didn't anticipate her
deadly line of attack.

she said things to me
that made me giddy
with excitement
and shudder in fear
all at once.

she wanted to delight me
and she said she would groom me in
the fine art of pleasurable satisfaction.

her penetrating stares made
me uncomfortable

but her body was a specimen

i only saw in fashion magazines.

a cougar cornered me

now i am at

her lust filled mercy.

<u>Letting Go</u>

By Sasha Davis

how to let go

of someone

that you allow

to consume you

use you

and

discard you anywhere

once it was

far from their heart.

how can you

allow the pained breaths

to escape

from your lungs

while you clutch on

your sheets wishing

they would envelop you?

how can you wake up

and look them

in their eyes

pretending as if you don't care?

when you know

you know

that he killed you

and you let him.

every tear was a choice

you chose

to drown in him

you let him

take you where

he needed you to go

you ran into him

full force

and damned yourself.

and now

you're left all alone

fearing to fall into

the arms of another

because you wonder if

that too is a lie.

Cleaning Out the Fridge

By r. A. bentinck

my mother would

always say that

whenever i come home

i am always cleaning out

the fridge.

she seems to have

a slight issue with

me wanting to

eat everything in sight.

so she loves to

describe my actions

as cleaning out her fridge.

i see it as just being hungry.

<u>Key</u>

By Sasha Davis

if our love

was like a padded lock

i'd search endlessly

for the key

and release you

from me.

My Whereabouts

By r. A. bentinck

silently i thought,
why does she need to
know everything?
my mother is always
up in my grill!

where are you going?

what time will you get back?

who are you going with?

are these good friends?

do you know the place
you are going to?

did you eat before you leave?
do you have on clean underwear?

my mother always wants

to know all the details

about where i'm going

and i am always reluctant

to divulge such information.

every time i have to go out

it's the recurring theme of

our conversations.

Strings Attached

By Sasha Davis

i wonder

how i look to you

from up there.

i wonder

if my frame looks

as vulnerable

as it does to me.

i wonder

if when you pull

my strings you can

see me wince in pain

and recoil in fear?

i wonder

if you can spot

the tears in my soul.

i wonder

if you even care

for you're

a master puppeteer.

I Made Her That Way

By r. A. bentinck

i was told that

my mother was the most

gentle of soul anyone can

get to know,

then i became a teen

and everyone pinned

the changes in her

on me.

she became a screamer,

a nagger,

a nervous wreck,

a detective,

an expert on selecting my friends,

the authority on young girls,

a specialist at detecting

dirty underwears and socks,

a dictator,

an expert on quoting the Bible,

a clean freak,

and a visionary.

there is never a dull moment

in our relationship these days.

i love my mom

but

i hate her newly developed attitudes.

Love Definitions

By Sasha Davis

love is

the beat of your heart.

the welcome

of your smile.

the aroma

of your scent.

the words

of honey

that drip from

your lips.

love is

pain and joy,

heartbreak and happiness,

177

acceptance and conformity,

youth and jubilee.

love is

smooth liquor

that slides through you

it joins with you

and you accept it.

for what temptation

is greater than love?

Girl Trouble

By r. A. bentinck

here she comes

once again

and

with her comes

bouts of nervousness,

loss of self-control,

heart palpitations

and dry, speechless mouth.

somehow she seems

to take all my common sense

with her when she leaves

and all she does

is brings heartbreak,

uncertainty

and tons of sweetness.

she is like

a gush of strong wind,

invariably she destroys

and break fragile things

in her path.

<u>Stay</u>

By Sasha Davis

i stayed

because i chose

to see a stable home

and not a sinking ship.

i stayed

because i decided not

to focus on

the troubled moments

and bask in the failures

of unrequited love.

Daddy

By r. A. bentinck

my best friend became

a daddy

and somehow that reality

has transformed my world

in ways i never envisioned.

my mother gave me

another lecturing today.

don't get anybody girl child

pregnant while you still

in school and

living in my house!

bring home good grades

not baby.

i'm not ready to become
a grandmother as yet
i sacrifice too much for you.

keep that thing in your pants,
do you hear me?

my best friend became
a teenage daddy
and somehow his newborn baby
has directly reformed my world
in ways, i never thought it could.

Pain

By Sasha Davis

bullet spaced breaths,

weary eyes

and

a heavy heart.

evidence of

the traces

you left

on my heart.

Light it Up

By r. A. bentinck

so i was sitting there

amongst the elder brethren

taking in

their words of wisdom

when the spliff made

its way to my position

in the wisdom circle.

with hands that shook

like the rustling leaves

i received the weed

and my lips

lost its smoking virginity.

i was blazing it up

just like the elders

while i listened

to their words of wisdom.

note to self,

remember to brush your teeth

before mom gets home.

This is the Best of My Heart

By Sasha Davis

the air that filled

my lungs,

the tears that

seeped over

the curves of my cheek.

this serves as

an escape

a passage of relief

a clear way of exiting

the pain entrapped

and harvested

all pouring out of

my soul.

this is my story

lyrics strung out

of my heart

this is

the pain,

the struggle,

the solitude,

my own personal recovery.

Heartbeat

By r. A. bentinck

she took

the lively rhythms

of my heart and

left me with

a gloomy heartbeat.

why does loss

beats this way?

what could

i have done differently

to make her stay?

why did i let her go?

why didn't she stay?

why does my heart

beat this way?

she took the lively rhythms

of my heartbeat

when she left.

Exhaustion

By Sasha Davis

i'm all dried out now

what are you going

to leech on

now that there is nothing left?

the pieces of my heart

have already all been sold off,

the vulnerability of my soul

has been thrust

into the spotlight,

the water from

the well inside me

has been exhausted,

the light inside me

has been used to illuminate others

so much that the supply

has dwindled to nothing.

nothing is left to give or take

so what are you going

to take from me?

now that my life has diminished

into nothing and

my eyes have filled over

the only offering i have left

that i seek no use for is

the breath in my body.

Flawless

By r. A. bentinck

i had the rugged looks
and the shabby booth,
she was like a rose
kissed by the morning dew-
flawless.

she was rich and lived
in the gated community,
i was poor and lived in
the notorious tenement yard
across the way.

somehow she fell for me.

despite our stark differences
i felt her genuine love for me,

i felt her kindness towards me,
i felt her appreciation for
my wild side.

despite the indifference from her
haughty friends she managed
to ignore it all and love me
unconditionally.

sasha davis and r. a. bentinck

Growth

By Sasha Davis

just as a flower opens up

to allow the sun

to provide it with warmth

you allowed me

to expose my petals to you.

i let you shine

on each one and

i absorbed every bit

of warmth, you radiated

it has been a while since

this wilting flower

had immersed itself

in light.

My Best Friend

By r. A. bentinck

i had

a best friend

yesterday.

today i caught him

with my girlfriend,

my heartbeat,

my honey bunny.

they were smooching

behind

the classroom door.

question?

are best friends

suppose

to do that?

seriously,
are they?

i had a best friend
yesterday
today, he stole
my girlfriend from
right under my nose.

<u>Girl</u>

By Sasha Davis

a girl is not an item

a sexual innuendo

a punching bag.

we are the carriers

of a nation

the source of strength

the pillars

of our community.

recognise our strength

or fall aside

with the rest

of the waste.

Changes

By r. A. bentinck

the beard

the boils

the bumps

the embarrassing acne

and

the unexpected wet dreams.

changing places

and expectations.

the girls,

the hormones

and uncertainties.

the criticisms

the lack of confidence

and the extra energies
and challenges.

mommy's expectations
and daddy's scolding.

these were
my ever-changing
teenage realities.

Wilted Patch

By Sasha Davis

she fluttered her eyes

so he followed

her trail

she never uttered

a word.

Miss

By r. A. bentinck

she must have been

heaven sent

that was my only

sensible conclusion.

i often wonder

why would heaven

send her to torture me?

to torture us?

why?

the classroom was

her catwalk

and the chalkboard

became a place where

she frequently poses.

why would the

God my mother

encouraged me to

serve every

morning and evening

do this to me?

why?

was He testing me?

she was my language teacher

and she was the finest

specimen of unspoiled beauty,

a prime example

of tenderness

with a voice that seeped

into the core of my soul.

why did she have

to be my teacher?

why did she have

to be older than me?

why do i feel

this way for her?

should i tell Miss

how i feel about her?

Someone New

By Sasha Davis

i met someone like you

he had the same smile

and

the same hidden intent

behind his eyes

but i ran instead

not trusting myself

with surrounding myself

with him too long.

205

I Can't Wait

By r. A. bentinck

i am just tired!

tired of all the chores,

tired of all the rules,

tired of all

the stupid curfews,

tired of the nagging,

tired of all

the instructions

about how to live

my life.

tired of the fussing

tired of the fighting.

i want to grow up

fast!

i want my own place,

i want to earn my own money,

set my own rules

and throw away

all curfews.

i want my adult life now!

i am tired of

this rule controlled living.

i need to be free.

Look How She Dances for Me

By Sasha Davis

she simply swayed along

to the base of the drums

enjoying the company

of her friends

the rush of the moment

simply exploring her surroundings

for a night

he wanted a victim

he seeded out his prey

she rushed outside

to catch her breath

overwhelmed

with the toxic air

he rushed outside

right into her

quickening his pace

another flower

was cut that night

and added

to a patch watered in hate.

Stress-Free Life

By r. A. bentinck

you have it easy,

my parents always

reminded me.

you have

'no chick, nor a child'

all you do is eat and sleep.

boy was they wrong,

they don't know

what it takes

to keep up with

the friends i have,

they don't know

what it takes

to fit into my elite clique,

they don't know
how much courage it takes
to speak to the girl
of my dreams,

they don't know the
boyhood schemes
i have to negotiate.
i have it easy?

no mama,
it's never easy out
here
you need to keep
praying for
your last boy child.

What is Passion

By Sasha Davis

passion would be our physical being
the thousands of thoughts that
run across our mind

passion would be the beat your heart makes
every time you breathe in life

passion would be you ceasing your very
being for that person who sparks
a fire inside of you

passion would be the constant overflow of
love you feel in every shared glance

passion would be the smile that graces your
face every time you catch

their familiar scent in the wind

passion would be the drive that pushes you

to do the most rebellious acts

it's in your children

it's in your eyes

and the eyes of your lover

passion would be you

Half Dead

By r. A. bentinck

yeah,

that's me,

half dead

being dragged

out of bed on another

school morning.

the repeated callings

i didn't want to hear

so my mom is here

dragging my always

tired body out

my comfy bed.

i was half dead.

yeah,

that was me

every school morning.

why do i have

to go to school any?

i'm half dead, anyway!

Wavelengths

By r. A. bentinck

listen,

i am convinced that adults

will never understand

us teens,

ever!

we are on two

different wavelengths.

they have outgrown

their teenage years,

they grew up in a different era.

and times have changed

so much.

the adults in my life

don't understand my struggles

and they never will

because we exist on

different wavelengths.

I'm different

By Sasha Davis

losing will soon become
this world's newfound source
to reap from.

the loss of our souls
birth the greatest warriors

the loss of familial ties
rear the vastest sinners

the loss of ourselves birthed
this generation

we walk around like
carbon copies
of one another

all screaming the same line.

Labels

By r. A. bentinck

somehow, without me
noticing it
i seem to have a lot of
girlfriends these days.

and for some unknown reason
the neighbourhood
think i am intimate
with all of them.

far from the truth.

now i've been branded
'the village ram,'
'the girl's man,'
'the stud,'

'the lover boy'

and because of this
some girls run from me,
while other girls flock me,
and many of the boys
are jealous of me.

Slut

By Sasha Davis

the clothes she wears

and the flutter of her lashes

some say

she's a born seductress

the swing of her hips

and the lies that roll of her lips

practiced skills for whoever she digs

her sight on

she's a born seductress

the river that adorns the top of her head

and the light ripples she makes with

the slight turn of her neck

her slick tongue and smooth nature

she's a born seductress not to be confused
with an average player

you follow the twinkle in her eyes
and the gleam reflected from her cheek
and you'll fall right into
this seductress final trick.

Anger Management

By r. A. bentinck

all my teachers

gave up on me.

so here i'm at

the guidance counsellor's

office.

i spent an hour there

and i didn't hear

a single word she said.

the principal told me

i had an anger problem

that i needed

to managed.

too many fights,

too many unexplained

outburst,

too many

unanswered question.

so i'm at the end of

my rope.

i was told,

get it together

or you are expelled!

Who are You?

By Sasha Davis

who gave the wolf permission

to prey on red riding hood?

who gave the ogre permission

to implore the darkest parts of

a child's mind?

who gave the witch permission

to deprive the world of beauty?

who gave you the right

to lie and swipe

the life of a mothers child?

they were not empty vessels

common occurrences

they were second chances

a bridge between faith and despair.

<u>Arrested</u>

By r. A. bentinck

it was a typical school day,
it was during school hour,
and we were out looking for
fun and adventure in
our school uniform.

a game of 8 ball pool
was too tempting to resist.

we were in the zone enjoying
game, after game, after game.
we were so caught up in
our game we didn't notice
the police standing at ease by
the shop door.
our body suddenly became

as rigid as the cuesticks in
our hands and our warm
perspiration drenched bodies
froze ice cold.

"why aren't you boys in school?"
the officer bellowed.
with our jaws on the ground and
fear in our bellies we couldn't
provide an answer.

so we were piled into
the back of the police vehicle
amongst the hardened criminals.
we were then paraded through the
streets for all our friends
and neighbours to see.

In the Valley

By r. A. bentinck

in the valley

way down in

the valley

of peer pressure,

family expectations,

society's prying eyes,

teachers' judgemental voices

in my head

and the thought of failing

constantly swirling

around in my head.

down in the valley

way down in

the valley

where the wrongs

seems right

and

all the right seems wrong.

where logical reasoning

isn't always logical.

in this valley, i struggle

to make sense

of life and living.

it's difficult to have

a clear-headed view

of this life, i am living,

right down here

in the valley.

First Love

By r. A. bentinck

i gave her everything i had
without her asking.

she stimulated feelings
in me that i never knew
existed before.

she brought lots of butterflies,
cold and shaky hands,
and an overactive imagination
that knows no limit.

she was my first love
and my first everything.

Teenage Years

By Sasha Davis

a collection of poetry

a binding of art

obstacles

heartache

rejection

awkwardness

all captured in through pictures in

the teenage years.

Pressures

By r. A. bentinck

the pressures come

from all directions,

peer pressure,

parent pressure,

exam pressure,

school pressure,

body image pressure,

relationship pressure,

money pressure,

time management pressure.

you name it,

its a pressure.

the list can

go on and on.

there is never a dull moment

in my teenage reality.

In the News Today

By r. A. bentinck

i saw it all
in the news today.

another adolescent boy
shot and killed
while committing a robbery,
another one is going to jail
for alleged murder,

another juvenile girl
was impregnated by her
relative and
the ministry of health
is worried about
teen obesity.
here i am

my mother's

clean as a whistle angel,

no arrest,

no crime committed,

no babies,

nor baby mamas

and yet still my parents

are stressing me the hell out!

enough already.

give me a break, please.

i could have been

another teenage statistic

on today's news

you know.

Growth Spurts

By r. A. bentinck

changes,

changes,

changes.

one day i realised

that my body started

do some freaky things.

hair started sprouting

from what seems like

everywhere.

my face is now a heaven for

pus-filled bumps,

and

there is a pungent smell

that's coming from my armpit

and less savoury places.

things are getting

longer and larger,

and am losing and

gaining weight like crazy.

changes,

changes,

changes.

Messed Up

By r. A. bentinck

they branded us

messed up,

because we are overexposed.

they say we are

the social media generation,

the selfie kings and queens,

the insensitive to violence beings.

we are the viral videos junkies

and the video challenge geeks.

but for some of us

we are just regular teens

who wants to live life

normally.

<u>Alone</u>

By r. A. bentinck

no one told me

there will be

days like this,

when i feel like shit

and

i feel all alone

despite being amongst

family and friends.

no one told me

there will me moments

like this when

i wish i were dead.

the pressures,

241

the uncertainties,

the doubts,

the fears,

the sadness,

the grief.

no one told me there

will be days like this

when i feel so all alone.

i am fed up,

i am disgusted,

i am confused,

i feel used.

seriously,

why didn't someone

told me there will be

days like this?

Twin Tale: Mary's Story

By r. A. bentinck

this was no immaculate conception,

mary and her boyfriend was

just fooling around.

she got pregnant.

the pressure that came with

that realisation was unimaginable.

hiding from her classmates,

thinking to herself:

"how would i finish school?"

"what would mum and dad say?"

"how would my boyfriend take

the news?"

she didn't know what to do.

to her boyfriend, she broke the news,

but he became a flip-flopping fool
and couldn't make up his mind.
so, she decided one day to
visit the doctor.

she said he forcibly evicted
the fetus from her womb and
after stuffing it into a jar with fluid,
he gave her the news.
"they were twins," she said calmly.
i saw the horror in her face
and felt her pain as
she grabbed her now vacant tummy.

"twins! twins! twins!"
she screamed softly.
he tears flowed like torrential rain.
she was feeling pain only a mother
could understand.

twins.

twins…

twins.

wasn't that her blessing?

why didn't the doctor advise

or counsel her?

i sat in her pregnant sadness

silently thinking,

and questions started popping up:

what's the purpose of the

hippocratic oath?

did the jar conceal

their silent screams?

what does the abortionist do with

these everyday memories?

what was he thinking while staring

into a young girl's eye?

does he have a daughter?

it wasn't immaculate conception,

but they were twins.

twins!

isn't that some kind of sin?

i am in no position to judge

but after all these years

i can still recall mary's story

and for me, the pain and sadness

never fade.

after all, they were twins.

247

Objects

By Sasha Davis

how do you look in
the eyes of the sun and
tell her she no longer has clouds
to keep her company?

how do you tell the rain
to stop from pouring?

how can you tell an infection
to stop from spreading?

you can't because it can not comprehend
the thought or feeling of loss
it does what it was designed
to do live
a soulless body has taken shelter

on this earth wandering around seeking

a home to grow where being a burden

upon someone else's shoulders isn't present

the conflict in mind is put to rest

and the chains of life have been written off.

Contradictions

By r. A. bentinck

one minute

they tell you to

grow up,

and in the next minute

they tell you to

act your age,

and enjoy your youth.

what do adults require from us?

can you be consistent

with your words of advice?

please,

we have enough to

deal with don't confuse

us any further.

Power

By Sasha Davis

black culture has sown its roots into

my very being

its grace has winded itself

to the electricity in my blood

the culture has consumed me

and the knowledge has birthed me anew

i've shed my skin of ignorance and

harsh denial

and chosen to walk the dust-ridden and

prejudicial avenues my ancestors marched

vacating my blind eye towards the apparent

rise of racism held within our own soil

the spirits of lions manifest in the soul of my

grandfather

his father

and his father before that

generations of strong black men who had to

succumb to the robbery of their childhood

and education

men who were forced to fall at the feet of

crooked and faulty laws

stripped of the rights they were entitled to

and cast out to rot in a world that only

allotted them dreams

tears escaped the eyes of our mothers

nourishing those held beneath them

quenching the thirst of the men they placed

above them

albeit watering a new generation cloaked

with the strength to come after it

the urgency of thousands of feet that ran

across dirt roads paved its existence to lead
others across
we are a force of power, labour, and hope
sowing the seeds of success to reap its fruits
and share with those around us so we can all
grow in the benefits

our people are a cascade of one heartbeat
regardless of the lightness of our skin
the difference in our upbringing
and the drift between our economic classes

we were all washed in the same struggle
lied before those who minimized us
rose above those who persecuted us
let the truth swallow us and wash us anew

so, that our endeavors propel us
to move forward

we are the bastions of those who are

to come after us

aligning ourselves with our mission to

mature into a breed different

from what anyone

has ever seen

our path is different

but the beauty sprinkled on the beads

leading up to there bind us together.

Expectations

By r. A. bentinck

if you fail

these examinations

your life is screwed.

if you don't get a university

education you will

flip burgers for

the rest of your life.

if you continue to behave

this way you will never

attract a suitable mate,

you will be left on

the shelf gathering dust.

our parents and teachers

always seems to paint
a bleak future for us
if we don't live up
to their expectations.

the terrifying pictures
they create leaves us
with sleepless nights,
and serious spells of
anxiety attacks.

Wanderer

By Sasha Davis

a soulless body has been thrust

upon the earth

searching to alleviate the adversities of

those surrounding it

pleasing those who displease it

uplifting those who dismantle it

relentlessly striving to remove the burden

found within itself

constantly stumbling upon each obstacle two

or three at a time

what loneliness it feels when the light shifts

to darkness

rooting out the pain within

stumbling from one hell to the next.

Dictatorship

By r. A. bentinck

what else can it be

but a dictatorship?

at home

they set my bedtime,

they set my wake up time,

they even advise me what

friends and company

i should keep.

at school

they inform me what time

to get there,

what time and which class

i should attend

they set the length of

my lunch and break time
and i get punished
when i flout the rules.

what else can this be?
i live in a dictatorship system.

<u>Untitled</u>

By Sasha Davis

i stumbled into hell

and fell right into you.

You Were Here Before?
(to our parents)

By r. A. bentinck

haven't you been through

this before?

haven't you been

thrust into this

intense situation where

physically and emotionally

everything is ever-changing.

shouldn't you be a little more

sympathetic?

haven't you been here before?

in your youthful day's

you know what it's like

to discover heartbreak,

anxiety,

low self-esteem

and peer pressure

that can reshape your life

forever.

haven't you been here before?

so, why can't you be

a little more empathetic?

Suicidal

By r. A. bentinck

i had an argument with

my mother for the thousandth time

this week.

in a family where am not

the only sibling i am expected

to do all the chores,

take all the blame

and it seems like

i am hated for no reason.

today is the last straw

i don't give a flying fuck!

i don't care anymore!

despite how hard i try

i still get the shitty end of the stick.

i just want to stab myself in the neck,

jump in front of a sand truck,

tie a plastic bag over my head,

god i wish i was dead!

i'm just tired of this shit!

The Poet

By Sasha Davis

witness the shame and the blood that

decorates each page

the courage it took to be able to pencil

down the truth closed off within

the vulnerable depths revealed to the

world to dissect, critique and analyze

my human persona used as the tool to

attract those who seek identification

establishing the emotional connection

created by the poet to fill in the adjacent

space between reader and writer

presented as an emotional puppeteer

vulnerability muse

however, the presentee is simply a poet.

The Fashion Police

By r. A. bentinck

they don't know

your family financial situation

but they want to dictate

to you what you should wear

and how long you should

wear it for.

don't get caught with

a shoe that was

last month's fashion,

they will crucify you

with criticism and

demeaning slurs.

you are forced to confirm

to their unrealistic standards

or face severe backlash.

it's a minefield out there
i tell you and if you are
not careful you get blown up
every day.

Lessons

By Sasha Davis

my heart has stopped

its natural process of

accepting bullshit.

The Outcast

By r. A. bentinck

i have bent over backwards

on countless instances

just to entertain them.

i have given them

the best of my lunch,

the last of my spending money,

and my prime attention

still, they wouldn't allow me

to be a part of the group.

their excuses are

am not tough enough,

i don't have the distinctive

hairstyle and texture,

and my boots aren't a brand name one

so i cannot be unanimously accepted.
to say i'm devastated is
a considerable understatement.

i have willingly given
these popular boys so much
yet i'm kept at bay because of a few
physical and material abnormalities.

Report Card Days

By r. A. bentinck

this is the time of

the school year where

it's a toss-up between

a plethora of punishment options

depending on the type of grade

i bring home.

the 90s and 80s are always celebrated,

the 70s brings words of encouragement

to press on,

but the 60s and 50s along

with failure can be brutal at times.

failure brings a total revoking of all

my teen privileges,

or the dreaded never-ending lecture

where i'm being told about
wasted potentials,
not holding up my end of the bargain,
and the importance of education
to my future development and success.

this is the time of the years when
my teacher pull out their comment sheet
and poor or substandard performances
are met with no mercy.

with report cards days
i have learned its best to just
perform well and save myself
lots of unnecessary heartaches.

Accidents

By Sasha Davis

"take it," she said carelessly
i witnessed her toss her heart willingly
to a boy who tugged at it until
she fell into him.

i saw her stumble down the same street
a number of times
staggering around potholes
and gliding over speed bumps.

ignoring the red signs that met her
at every corner and
tuning her view to avenues of green lights.

i planted seeds of warning
along each step downward

alerting her senses

relentlessly trying to divert her attention

persuading her to yield.

but i saw her speed up and head

onto a street that had no light

to illuminate the deepest creeks

held along the street

she then proceeded to press

her feet down on the pedal

accelerating directly into a wall.

the seatbelt that was draped around her

for protection cut into her throat

and came undone slashing her face

there she lay broken in pieces in her car

yet the wall remained unmoving.

Invisible

By r. A. bentinck

somehow despite how often

she passes by

she doesn't notice me.

when she gets close

my emotions erupt

her name propels me

into a fit a nervous frenzy,

still, she doesn't notice me.

i have parted

the emotional seas

for her umpteen times,

i have walked on razor blades

just to get a glimpse of her

yet, she doesn't see me.

what more do i need to do?
what more do i need to master?
what more do i need to say
just to get her to see me?

somehow despite what she
does to me in her eyes
i'm just not visible.

Outspoken Outlet

By Sasha Davis

witness the shame and

the blood that decorates each page.

the courage it took to be able

to pencil down the truth closed off within.

the vulnerable depths revealed to

the world to dissect,

critique and analyze my human persona

used as the tool to attract

those who seek identification.

establishing the emotional connection

created by the poet to fill in

the adjacent space between

the reader and writer.

presented as an emotional puppeteer

vulnerability muse, however

the presentee is simply a poet.

Survivors

By r. A. bentinck

despite what they say,

despite how it looks,

as teens, we are always resilient.

we are stronger than

they perceive us to be.

we are wiser beyond our years.

we will always find ways

to grow and develop.

i survived,

our parents survived,

they survived,

we survived,

and

you will survive

these teenage years too.

About the Authors

Sasha davis and r. a. Bentinck

Sasha Davis is a recent, esteemed graduate of the prestigious Bishop Michael Eldon School located in Freeport, Bahamas. She is currently in pursuit of her bachelor's degree in biology at the University of Tampa. Being raised on the island of Grand Bahama by two devoted parents Eddison and Malinda Davis,

281

the art of writing was always a passion she sought throughout her primary and secondary career of school.

She was finally awarded the opportunity to publish her poems in collaboration with Mr. Bentinck, her former Art and Design teacher in the book entitled, The Flaws in Our Teen: An Unfiltered Look at the Teenage Years Through Poetry. During her free time, you'll find her doodling in a sketchbook, browsing through the years of past historic figures, and fidgeting over her latest novel.

r. A. bentinck is the author of *Of all the Lilies* (2017), *Underneath the Poetry series* (2017-18), *Seduced* and *The Seductive Collection* (2019). He is an Educator and Artist who is presently focusing on his self-publishing business while tutoring part-time at the E.R. Burrowes School of Art as a painting and drawing Tutor. He is a graduate of the University of Guyana with a B. A. Degree in Fine Arts and a Diploma in Education (Administration).

www.ingramcontent.com/pod-product-compliance
Lightning Source LLC
LaVergne TN
LVHW091248080426
835510LV00007B/165